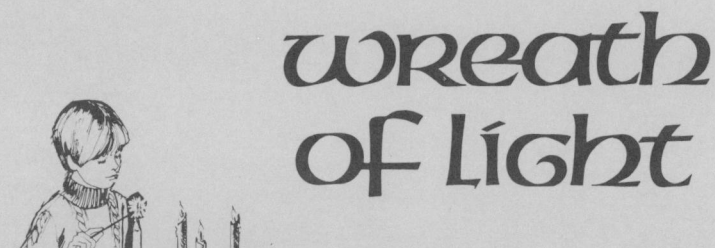

Wreath of Light

Devotions for Families Using the Advent Wreath

by Nancy Vignec

AUGSBURG PUBLISHING HOUSE

Minneapolis, Minnesota 55415

ISBN 0-8066-1727-6

Scripture quotations are from the Revised Standard Version of the Bible, © 1946, 1952, 1971, and are used by permission.

Copyright © 1979 **Augsburg Publishing House**
All rights reserved
Manufactured in the United States of America

Contents

USING THE ADVENT WREATH   4

THE CANDLE OF WAITING   6

THE CANDLE OF JOY   14

THE CANDLE OF PRAISE   22

THE CANDLE OF FAITH   30

HYMNS   38

Using the Advent Wreath

SURROUNDED BY WINTER DARKNESS we gather in candlelight. Candles on a cake mean it's time to celebrate a birthday. A candlelight dinner promises intimate conversation. Altar candles remind us of God's presence.

Four candles on a wreath mean it's Advent, a time to prepare for the celebration of Jesus' birth at Christmas. It is a time to think about his grace and forgiveness in our daily lives and to look forward to his coming at the end of time.

Many families find their Advent preparation and meditation is enriched by using an Advent wreath in their homes. Each day during the first week of Advent the family lights one candle on their wreath. Two candles are lighted the second week, three the third week, and all four the fourth week. Each week the family's devotions focus on a theme suggested by Advent scripture texts and hymns. In this booklet the weekly themes are **waiting, joy, praise,** and **faith.**

Colors for the Advent candles vary from home to home. Many families use blue candles as a symbol of hope. Others use purple, the color of royalty, as a reminder of Jesus the king. Red or white candles are also used.

Before your family begins the Advent devotions you will want to decide who will light the candles and who will snuff them. An older child might be asked to find the Bible verse and read it, or to choose the song the family will sing and find it in songbooks or hymnals you may have at home. Children may also read the devotion or lead the prayer.

At times you may wish to discuss family experiences related to a day's meditation. Or you might include your family's particular concerns with the printed prayer.

Before the concluding prayer some families attach paper stars to their wreaths. Written on the stars are the names of those for whom the family prays. These prayer stars mark the daily approach of Christmas while focusing attention on our Christian love for others.

The period just before or after a meal is often set aside for family devotions, and the dining room or kitchen table seems a natural place to gather. But your family may find another time or place that is better for you. Some families meet in a different room each week, with a child or parent serving as that week's "keeper of the Advent wreath."

Your family may begin using the Advent wreath and the devotions in this booklet four Sundays before Christmas, which is the first day of Advent, and continue through the day before Christmas Eve. Then the Christmas Eve devotion may be read.

The Candle of Waiting

FIRST WEEK **Sunday**

(Choose one person to light the first candle. Other suggestions for family participation may be found in the introduction.)

Read (as the candle is lighted): We call the first candle on our wreath "Waiting," because Advent is a time of *waiting*.

**Lead me in thy truth, and teach me,
  for thou art the God of my salvation;
  for thee I wait all the day long** (Psalm 25:5).

Mother carried a big box marked "Advent and Christmas" into the living room.

"Hooray!" shouted Tommy. "It's time to decorate for Christmas!"

"Christmas is coming soon," said mother. "We have only four more weeks to wait."

"Do we have to wait that long to set up our Christmas decorations?" asked Susan.

"All four weeks of Advent does seem like a long time," said mother. "But let's try to wait a little while. Today I am going to unwrap only one thing from this box."

"What is it?" asked Tommy.

"This is the Advent wreath your Aunt Mary gave us," answered mother. "And here are the candles."

"Oh, I remember," said Susan. "We have four candles and there are four weeks in Advent. We light the candles to show how long it is until Christmas."

"And each time we light them we think about what God wants us to learn while we're waiting for Christmas. If we're going to celebrate Jesus' birth, we need to spend some time each day remembering the special gift God gave us when Jesus was born that first Christmas long ago."

(If your family is unfamiliar with using the Advent wreath, you may want to discuss its use now.)

Sing: First stanza of "Your little ones, dear Lord, are we" (page 38).

Pray: Dear Jesus, sometimes we think we can't wait until Christmas. Help us to use the four weeks of Advent to learn more about you. Amen.

(Family waits quietly until candle is snuffed.)

FIRST WEEK   **Monday**

(The candle of **waiting** will be lighted later. You will need a watch or clock with a second hand for today's devotion.)

Sing: First stanza of "Your little ones, dear Lord, are we" (page 38).

Read: Do you know how long one minute is? Today we're going to wait one minute before we light the Advent candle. All of you close your eyes and put your hands on the table. When you think one minute is over, lift one finger.

(After one minute.) When we are waiting even a minute can be long. Let's open our eyes and light the candle of waiting. (Candle may be lighted.)

"Behold, the days are coming, says the Lord, when I will fulfil the promise I made to the house of Israel" (Jeremiah 33:14).

While we are waiting to celebrate Christmas, we remember the people of Israel who lived before Jesus was born. We think about the long years they waited for God to send Jesus the promised Savior.

Pray: Dear God, thank you for giving us Jesus, the Savior the Israelites awaited so long. Amen.

Tuesday   **FIRST WEEK**

Read (as the candle is lighted): During Advent we are **waiting** and getting ready to celebrate Jesus' birth.

You are not lacking any spiritual gift, as you wait for the revealing of our Lord Jesus Christ (1 Corinthians 1:7).

"Would you like to help me set up these figures from our nativity scene?" asked mother.

"Yes," said Tommy. "But couldn't we have the shepherds and Wise Men too? Mary and Joseph will look lonely by themselves. And we need baby Jesus."

"Soon we'll set out all the figures," said mother. "While we're waiting let's think about Mary and Joseph.

"Before you were born your father and I bought a new crib and baby clothes. When it was time for Jesus' birth Mary and Joseph were far from their own home. They couldn't bring along a crib and clothes for Jesus. But they were ready for him in the most important way. They were ready to love him."

Sing: Second stanza of "Your little ones, dear Lord, are we" (page 38).

Pray: Dearest Jesus, as we think of Mary and Joseph waiting for your birth, we think of their love for you. Help us to remember the most important gift we have is love. Amen.

FIRST WEEK   **Wednesday**

Read (as the candle is lighted): The first candle of Advent reminds us we are **waiting** to welcome Jesus.

Sing: Third stanza of "Your little ones, dear Lord, are we" (page 38).

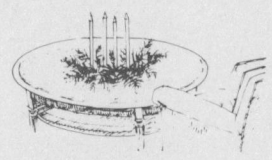

May the Lord make you increase and abound in love (1 Thessalonians 3:12a).

Tommy was helping mother with the baking. Susan and father were arranging furniture in the guest room. They were getting ready for grandma and grandpa.

The ringing telephone interrupted their work. Carol Thompson was hurt. The Thompsons needed them to watch the other children while Carol was rushed to the hospital.

Quickly everyone thought of a way to help. Tommy found books to read to the little ones. Susan gathered toys for them. As the family hurried out the front door, they almost bumped into grandpa and grandma!

Pray: O Lord, while we are waiting to welcome you, show us how to love others by being kind and helpful. Amen.

Thursday   FIRST WEEK

Read (as the candle is lighted): We call this candle **waiting**, because Jesus told us to wait and watch for him.

Watch therefore, for you do not know on what day your Lord is coming (Matthew 24:42).

Leaving his toys on the floor, Jimmy ran to the window and peered out into the dark night. Jimmy was waiting and watching. His father was gone on a long trip. Jimmy knew he would come home again, but he didn't know which day. Maybe today he would come!

Jimmy wanted to be ready. As soon as his father walked in the door Jimmy wanted to give him a big hug and say, "Dad, I'm so glad you are home!" And Jimmy knew his father would take him up in his arms and hug him too, because he knew his father loved him.

Pray: Dear Jesus, we wait and watch eagerly for you. Keep our love for you strong so we will be ready for your coming. Amen.

Sing: Second stanza of "Your little ones, dear Lord, are we" (page 38).

FIRST WEEK **Friday**

Read (as the candle is lighted): The candle of **waiting** reminds us we are waiting to celebrate Jesus' birthday.

Sing: Third stanza of "Your little ones, dear Lord, are we" (page 38).

"Lo, I am with you always..." (Matthew 28:20b).

"This is going to be the best birthday party we've ever had for grandma!" exclaimed Wendy.

"For as long as I can remember, grandma has come to our house to celebrate her birthday," said mother. "It's been wonderful every year."

"Yes, but she used to live so far away. I always felt a little sad on her birthday knowing she would have to leave again after a few days. Then I would have to wait a whole year to see her again. Now that grandma has moved into the apartment down the street, I can see her every day, and on her birthday too!"

Pray: Loving Jesus, we are waiting for your birthday at Christmas, but we are glad you are always with us. Amen.

Saturday FIRST WEEK

Read (as the candle is lighted): **Waiting.** During Advent we learn about waiting patiently.

The Lord is not slow about his promise as some count slowness, but is forbearing . . . (2 Peter 3:9a).

What a lot of waiting we do during Advent! When we buy Christmas gifts for our family and friends we have to wait and wait in long lines. And after we've wrapped the gifts we must mark them: Do not open till Christmas. We'd like to give our gifts right away, but we have to wait.

God is waiting too. And what wonderful gifts he has for all of us! God is waiting for all people everywhere to become his. God loves each of us. He wants to give everyone the gifts of his love and forgiveness. And he wants us all to love him more than anyone or anything else.

Pray: Heavenly Father, thank you for waiting patiently for us to love you. Teach us to be patient and loving too. Amen.

Sing: Third stanza of "Your little ones, dear Lord, are we" (page 38).

SECOND WEEK   Sunday

Read (as the candles are lighted): Today we begin the second week of Advent. We light the candle of *waiting* to remind us of God's people waiting for the Savior, Jesus, to be born. The second candle on our wreath is called "Joy," because Jesus' coming makes us *joyful.*

Sing: First stanza of "Joy to the world" (page 38).

"Behold, I send my messenger to prepare the way before me . . . the messenger of the covenant in whom you delight . . ." (Malachi 3:1).

Every week each child in Miss Decker's classroom was chosen to help in a special way. One child emptied the pencil sharpener, another helped pass out papers, another cleaned the erasers. There was a classroom task for everyone.

The classroom messenger carried Miss Decker's messages to other teachers or to the office. If the class was going to another room for a program or a movie, Miss Decker would send the messenger to make sure everything was ready.

God has chosen people to be his messengers too. Long ago his messengers, the prophets, were sent to tell people what God wanted them to do and to remind them of God's promises, especially the promise that Jesus would come to be our Savior.

When Jesus was a man, ready to begin his work of teaching and healing, God sent a messenger, John the Baptist, so people would be ready for Jesus. Many people were filled with joy when they heard John the Baptist say, "The kingdom of heaven is at hand," because this message meant God's promised Savior, Jesus, was coming soon.

Pray: Dear God, thank you for those who bring the joyous good news about your Son Jesus. Amen.

SECOND WEEK   **Monday**

Read (as the candles are lighted): Advent is a time of **waiting** and a time of **joy.**

In those days came John the Baptist, preaching in the wilderness of Judea, "Repent, for the kingdom of heaven is at hand" (Matthew 3:1-2).

God sent John the Baptist to help people be ready for Jesus. He told people to repent, to be sorry for their sins, for the wrong things they had done.

Sometimes it's not easy to say "I'm sorry." But if the person we have hurt loves us, it's easier to ask forgiveness. Jesus came to earth to tell us God loves and forgives us, even when we do something wrong. Knowing about God's love and forgiveness fills us with joy!

Pray: Heavenly Father, we know we should be loving and kind all the time, but sometimes we do things that are wrong. Thank you for the joy of being loved and forgiven. Amen.

Sing: Second stanza of "Joy to the world" (page 38).

Tuesday SECOND WEEK

Read (as the candles are lighted): **Waiting.** We think of Mary waiting for Jesus to be born. **Joy.** Our Savior Jesus brings us joy.

Mary said, "My soul magnifies the Lord, and my spirit rejoices in God my Savior..." (Luke 1:46-47).

A mother feels great joy when she finds out she is going to have a child. The family rejoices because a new baby will be born.

After the angel told her she would have a son, Mary was joyful. Perhaps she thought about the happiness little children bring their parents. She may have looked forward to the day her son would hug her and say, "Mama, I love you!"

But Mary's joy over this new baby was special because Jesus is special. He is God's Son, the Savior Mary's people had awaited many long years. Jesus brought joy, not only to his own family, but to all the people of the world.

Sing: Third stanza of "Joy to the world" (page 39).

Pray: Dearest Jesus, we rejoice because you came to save all people. Thank you for being our Savior. Amen.

SECOND WEEK **Wednesday**

Read (as the candles are lighted): The first candle is called **waiting.** We call the second candle **joy** because we rejoice over all God does for us.

Sing: Second stanza of "Joy to the world" (page 38).

The Lord has done great things for us;
  we are glad ...
Who goes forth weeping ...
  shall come home with shouts of joy ... (Psalm 126:3, 6).

Everyone in the town was worried. A young boy was lost in the woods. Some people had gone out to look for him. They promised to ring the church bell as soon as they found the boy.

All night long the townspeople listened for the bell. In the morning they looked at each other sadly. The boy was still missing.

Suddenly they heard the church bell ringing joyously. The boy who had been lost was found!

Pray: Dear God, we would be lost and unhappy without you. You make us joyful by loving us. Help us to live as your people. Amen.

Thursday SECOND WEEK

Read (as the candles are lighted): This is the candle of **waiting**. This is the candle of **joy.**

I thank my God in all my remembrance of you, always in every prayer of mine for you making my prayer with joy (Philippians 1:3-4).

A young woman moved to a city far away from her home. Her new neighbors and the people in her church were kind and friendly to her, but she missed her old friends. Sometimes she felt very lonely.

One day a letter came. Inside was a picture of the young woman's friends at the party they had given her before she moved away. One of her friends had written on the picture: God loves you and we love you!

The young woman's eyes filled with tears of joy.

Sing: Third stanza of "Joy to the world" (page 39).

Pray: O Lord, thank you for the people who make us joyful. Show us how we can bring joy to others. Amen.

SECOND WEEK   **Friday**

Read (as the candles are lighted): **Waiting. Joy.** God's people are waiting for the joy of being with him.

And then he will send out the angels, and gather his elect. (Mark 13:27a).

Have you ever been to a reunion? Maybe this Christmas aunts and uncles and cousins will be coming to your house. Maybe your family will go to your grandparents' home. Or maybe you will celebrate Christmas with special friends. A reunion is a joyful time, a chance to be with friends and family we haven't seen in a long while.

One day our lives and the world as we know it will come to an end. We may feel frightened sometimes thinking of all the changes that might happen when the end comes. But Jesus has promised us that when the world ends all his people will be gathered together with him. What a joyous reunion that will be!

Pray: Dear Jesus, thank you for the joy of knowing we are your people always—even when the world comes to an end. Amen.

Sing: Third stanza of "Joy to the world" (page 39).

Saturday   **SECOND WEEK**

Read (as the candles are lighted): We call this candle **waiting** and this candle **joy.**

Sing: First stanza of "Joy to the world" (page 38).

**The Lord . . . will rejoice over you with gladness,
    he will renew you in his love;
he will exult over you with loud singing** (Zephaniah 3:17).

A mother and father were watching their children. Sometimes the children were not good playmates. A brother might say something unkind. A sister might hurt her brother. These things made the parents sad. Because they loved their children, the mother and father wanted the children to be happy together.

Today the children shouted happily to each other as they played. And their watching parents smiled with joy.

Pray: Heavenly Father, we know you love us all the time, even when the things we do make you unhappy. But we want to bring you joy! Help us show our love for you by being kind and thoughtful with others. Amen.

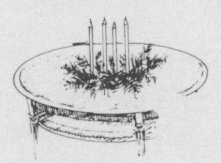

The Candle of Praise

Sunday   **THIRD WEEK**

Praise the Lord from the heavens . . .
Praise him, sun and moon,
   praise him, all you shining stars! (Psalm 148:1, 3).

Read (as the candles are lighted): Today is the third Sunday in Advent, so this week we light three candles on our wreath. The first candle is called *waiting* to remind us we are waiting to celebrate Jesus' birth at Christmas. We call the second candle *joy* because Jesus came to bring us the joy of love and forgiveness. Our third candle is named "Praise." We *praise* God for all he has given us.

When the candles on the Advent wreath had been snuffed, father said, "Let's make this a special evening for praising God. In a few minutes we're going to church for the choir concert. On the way let's look and listen for sights and sounds of praise."

As they rode down the street in their car, the children pointed out several windows glowing in candlelight. They said families in these homes might be gathered around an Advent wreath, praising God in songs and prayers. Other houses were brightly lighted with strings of outdoor lights. The children thought these were lights of praise too, because they remind us of the glory of God that shown at Christmas.

Mother talked about the words of praise on the Christmas cards the family had received. "Glory to God in the highest!" "Hosanna! The Savior is born!"

It was very dark when the family got out of their car in the church parking lot. Everyone looked up into the darkness, hoping to see some stars. The clear night sky was filled with starlight. Tonight even the heavens were praising God.

Pray: Dear God, help us see and hear the sights and sounds of praise around us. We want to join in and praise you too! Amen.

Sing: First stanza of "Give to our God immortal praise" (page 39).

THIRD WEEK **Monday**

Read (as the candles are lighted): **Waiting. Joy. Praise.** We praise God for the gift of Jesus our Savior.

"The Son of man will be delivered into the hands of men, and they will kill him . . . (Mark 9:13a).

"Ouch!" cried Susan. "Holly makes a pretty decoration, but I'd rather use something that wasn't so prickly."

"The thorniness is why people began using holly during Advent and Christmas," said mother. "Those sharp spiny leaves remind us of the crown of thorns Jesus wore when he died on the cross. The red holly berries remind us of his blood."

Sing: Second stanza of "Give to our God immortal praise" (page 40).

During Advent we praise God for the gift of Jesus, the Child who was born that first Christmas. We also remember that Jesus grew to be a man who suffered and died to save us from sin and death. Our Savior Jesus gave his life for us.

Pray: Jesus, you love us so much you were willing to die for us. We praise you, our loving Savior. Amen.

Tuesday

THIRD WEEK

Read (as the candles are lighted): These three candles remind us that Advent is a time for **waiting,** for **joy,** for **praise.**

I will praise the Lord as long as I live;
  I will sing praises to my God while I have being . . .
The Lord lifts up those who are bowed down (Psalm 146:2, 8).

Sing: Second stanza of "Give to our God immortal praise" (page 40).

For their Advent visit to the hospital the children's choir had planned a special song for the man in room 308. Mr. Peters had been a patient for such a long time many children had made friends with him. But when they came to his room, their friend was gone.

"I have good news for you," said the nurse. "Mr. Peters got better. He is home with his family."

Mr. Peters wasn't there to hear the song they had chosen for him. But the children sang in thanks and praise to God for making their friend well.

Pray: Heavenly Father, we praise and thank you for keeping us healthy and for healing those who are ill. Amen.

THIRD WEEK   **Wednesday**

Read (as the candles are lighted): **Waiting. Joy. Praise.** We praise Jesus, the King of Kings.

"Blessed is the King who comes in the name of the Lord! Peace in heaven and glory in the highest!" (Luke 19:38).

The kings and queens and rulers of this world may seem strong and powerful to us. When they give orders, other people obey. They may live in huge palaces with many servants. They may be rich and own many wonderful things.

Sing: Third stanza of "Give to our God immortal praise" (page 40).

During Advent we sing hymns praising the King of Kings. We see banners or posters showing crowns. These songs and pictures remind us Jesus is the king of heaven and earth. Everything in the world is his. Jesus is the king and ruler in our lives. We obey him because he loves us and we love him. We praise him because the power of his love is greater than anything.

Pray: Loving Jesus, we praise you our King and Savior! Amen.

Thursday

THIRD WEEK

Read (as the candles are lighted): We are God's **waiting** people. We welcome him with **joy.** We **praise** him.

**Blessed are the people who know the festal shout,
   who walk, O Lord, in the light of thy countenance**
(Psalm 89:15).

The children in Jimmy's Sunday school class liked to sing. Sometimes the singing was so loud it was more like shouting. Jimmy's teacher liked quiet voices and beautiful music, but she said, "When we love God and want to show our joy in him, even shouting can be praising."

One day Jimmy brought a friend with him to class. When the singing started the new boy joined in.

"You know our songs," said Jimmy's teacher. "I'm glad Christians everywhere love to praise God. Praising God with others reminds us we are people God has chosen to be his own."

Sing: Third stanza of "Give to our God immortal praise" (page 40).

Pray: Dear God, we praise and thank you for making us your people. Amen.

THIRD WEEK   **Friday**

Read (as the candles are lighted): God is **waiting** for all people to become his. He wants us to tell others of our **joy** in him. We **praise** God before all people.

Sing: Third stanza of "Give to our God immortal praise" (page 40).

> **The Lord will cause righteousness and praise to spring forth before all the nations** (Isaiah 61:11b).

One family has a colorful Advent wreath. Around the outside of the wreath are tiny flags. Each is the flag of a different nation. These flags remind us that God wants all people to hear us praise him.

Every day of Advent the family chooses one of the flags from the wreath. They pray for the missionaries and pastors of that nation, that the people living there may hear the good news of God's love for them.

During Advent the family saves money for a gift to the people of one of these countries. The money is used to buy food or clothing for people who need help. The family's Advent gift shows God's love for all people.

Pray: O Lord, help us praise you in all we do and say, so all people may know about your love. Amen.

Saturday   **THIRD WEEK**

(Candle of **waiting** and candle of **joy** may be lighted. Read as third candle is lighted): God wants us to be full of **praise.**

Rejoice always, pray constantly, give thanks in all circumstances . . . hold fast what is good . . . (1 Thessalonians 5:16-18, 21b).

At the supper table Tommy exclaimed, "I like being in Miss Decker's class! She doesn't nag at us. She talks about things that make me happy."

"I enjoy talking to Miss Decker," said father. "Sometimes she has to tell us your school work or the way you are treating other children isn't what it should be. But she always has a word of praise for you."

"I guess Miss Decker is so busy thinking about good things she doesn't have much time for complaining," said mother.

Sing: First stanza of "Give to our God immortal praise" (page 39).

Pray: Dear Jesus, thank you for the people whose words make us happy. Help us speak kindly to others. Make us full of praise for you. Amen.

The Candle of Faith

FOURTH WEEK — **Sunday**

(Candles will be lighted in a little while.)

Read: For four weeks now we've been watching for signs that Christmas is coming soon. We've waited for the first Christmas cards. We've watched for the first Christmas lights and decorations. We've sniffed eagerly for the smells of evergreens and Christmas baking. And each week we've lighted one more candle on our Advent wreath.

(Candles may now be lighted.) We light the candle of *waiting,* the candle of *joy,* and the candle of *praise.* The fourth candle is called *faith.* We remember the faith of the people of Israel.

Long ago the people of Israel were watching for signs that Jesus was coming soon. They had faith in signs from God. God sent his messengers, the prophets, to tell people the promises he made about Jesus, the King and Savior who was coming.

But you, O Bethlehem Ephrathah,
   who are little to be among the clans of Judah,
from you shall come forth for me
   one who is to be ruler in Israel (Micah 5:2a).
   Therefore the Lord himself will give you a sign. Behold, a young woman shall conceive and bear a son, and shall call his name Immanuel (Isaiah 7:14).

Immanuel means "God with us." We believe that Jesus is "God with us," because he is God's Son.

Sing: First stanza of "Oh, come, oh, come, Emmanuel" (page 40).

Pray: Dear God, give us faith and hope like the people of Israel who waited for Immanuel, your Son Jesus. Amen.

FOURTH WEEK   **Monday**

Read (as the candles are lighted): **Waiting. Joy. Praise. Faith.** We remember the people of Israel who had faith in God's promise to send a Savior.

These all died in faith, not having received what was promised . . . (Hebrews 11:13a).

During Advent a Sunday school class decorated a Jesse tree to remind them of those who lived long before Jesus was born. A six-pointed Star of David was on the tree as a reminder of David, the great king of Israel. The Jesse tree is named after David's father, Jesse.

The class made paper chains for their Jesse tree. Names were written on the strips of paper before they were pasted together. Some of the names were Abraham, Isaac, Jacob, Judah. These people died before Jesus was born, but they told their children about God's promise. They had faith that God would send Jesus the Savior, and they passed their faith on to others.

Sing: Second stanza of "Oh, come, oh, come, Emmanuel" (page 40).

Pray: Heavenly Father, thank you for those who teach us about you and pass on their faith to us. Amen.

Tuesday   FOURTH WEEK

Sing (before the candles are lighted): Third stanza of "Oh, come, oh, come, Emmanuel" (page 40).

Read (as the candles are lighted): We are God's **waiting** people. He brings us **joy.** We **praise** him. We put our **faith** and trust in him.

For with God nothing will be impossible (Luke 1:37).

There were many things for Mary to think about after the angel told her she was going to have a baby. She was excited about being a mother. She was joyful because this baby would be the Savior God had promised.

But Mary was also afraid. She may have been only 12 or 14 years old. Perhaps she was worried about how to be a good mother for such an important baby as Jesus.

Mary was chosen to be Jesus' mother because of her faith in God. She trusted God more than anyone or anything else. Mary knew God would help her.

Pray: O God, keep our faith, our hope, and our trust strong in you. Amen.

FOURTH WEEK   **Wednesday**

Read (as the candles are lighted): Light only the candle of **waiting.** The light from one candle is not very strong. Now light the candles of **joy, praise** and **faith.** The light of all four candles together is stronger.

It is good for us to be with others who believe in God. They can strengthen our faith.

"And blessed is she who believed that there would be a fulfillment of what was spoken to her from the Lord" (Luke 1:45).

After the angel talked with Mary about the baby Jesus, Mary ran to her cousin Elizabeth's house. Elizabeth had faith in God. Mary knew Elizabeth would understand all the angel had told her about Jesus.

As soon as Elizabeth saw Mary she knew what had happened. She knew Mary's baby would be Jesus the Savior. And Elizabeth was thankful Mary had believed the angel's message from God.

Pray: O Lord, thank you for those who share our faith in you. Amen.

Sing: Second stanza of "Oh, come, oh, come, Emmanuel" (page 40).

Thursday

Fourth Week

Read (as the candles are lighted): **Waiting. Joy. Praise. Faith.** God wants us to have faith in him and obey him.

God chose a good man to be Mary's husband. Then God sent an angel to tell Joseph what to do. The angel said,

"Joseph, son of David, do not fear to take Mary your wife, for that which is conceived in her is of the Holy Spirit; she will bear a son, and you shall call his name Jesus, for he will save his people from their sins" (Matthew 1:20b-21).

Joseph had faith in God. He believed what the angel told him. When the baby was born, Joseph named him Jesus. Because Joseph believed in God and obeyed him, God showed Joseph how to be a kind and loving husband for Mary and a good father to Jesus.

Sing: First stanza of "Oh, come, oh, come, Emmanuel" (page 40).

Pray: Heavenly Father, give us strong faith so we obey you and let you show us how to live. Amen.

Fourth Week **Friday**

Sing (before candles are lighted): Third stanza of "Oh, come, oh, come, Emmanuel" (page 40).

Read (as the candles are lighted: God's people were **waiting** for the promised Savior. We welcome Jesus with **joy** and **praise.** We have **faith** that he is the Son of God.

When Jesus was a man preaching and teaching and healing, people thought he might be a prophet or teacher sent from God. They saw those Jesus healed. They heard the wise words Jesus said.

But most people did not understand Jesus was the Son of God. They did not know he was the King and Savior God had promised.

One day some men asked Jesus,
"Are you he who is to come, or shall we look for another?"
(Matthew 11:3).

We are thankful we know the answer to this question. God has given us faith in Jesus. We know Jesus is our King and Savior, the Son of God.

Pray: Dear God, thank you for giving us faith in your Son Jesus. Amen.

Christmas Eve

Read (as the candles are lighted): Tomorrow is Christmas Day. As we light the candles on our wreath, we know our four weeks of Advent **waiting** are nearly over. We can celebrate Christmas with **joy** and **praise** because of the **faith** God has given us.

Sing:
I am so glad each Christmas Eve,
The night of Jesus' birth!
Then like the sun the star shone forth,
And angels sang on earth.

The little child in Bethlehem,
He was a king indeed!
For he came down from heav'n above
To help a world in need.

Read: Let's read the story of Jesus' birth (Luke 2:1-20).

Pray: Dear God, the years of waiting for the promised Savior are over! We rejoice with the shepherds. We join the angels' songs of praise. Give us faith to live always as your people. Amen.

Hymns

(A different hymn stanza could be sung each day, or you may choose to repeat the first stanza throughout the week. Some families may prefer to sing a favorite hymn not printed here.)

1 **Your little ones, dear Lord, are we,**
And come your lowly bed to see;
Enlighten ev'ry soul and mind,
That we the way to you may find.

2 With songs we hasten you to greet,
And kiss the ground before your feet
Oh, blessed hour, oh, sweetest night
That gave you birth, our soul's delight.

3 Oh, draw us wholly to you, Lord,
And to us all your grace accord;
True faith and love to us impart,
That we may hold you in our heart.

1 **Joy to the world, the Lord is come!**
Let earth receive its King;
Let ev'ry heart prepare him room
And heav'n and nature sing,
And heav'n and nature sing,
And heav'n, and heav'n and nature sing.

2 No more let sin and sorrow grow
Nor thorns infest the ground;
He comes to make his blessings flow
Far as the curse is found,
Far as the curse is found,
Far as, far as the curse is found.

Hymns

3   Joy to the earth, the Savior reigns!
    Let all their songs employ,
    While fields and floods,
       rocks, hills, and plains
    Repeat the sounding joy,
    Repeat the sounding joy,
    Repeat, repeat the sounding joy.

1   **Give to our God immortal praise!**
    Mercy and truth are all his ways;
    Wonders of grace to God belong;
    Repeat his mercies in your song.

Hymns

2. He sent his Son with pow'r to save
   From guilt and darkness and the grave.
   Wonders of grace to God belong;
   Repeat his mercies in your song.

3. Give to the Lord of lords renown;
   The King of kings with glory crown.
   His mercies ever shall endure
   When lords and kings are known no more!

1. **Oh, come, oh, come, Emmanuel,**
   And ransom captive Israel,
   That mourns in lonely exile here
   Until the Son of God appear.
   Rejoice! Rejoice! Emmanuel
   Shall come to you, O Israel.

2. Oh, come, strong Branch of Jesse, free
   Your own from Satan's tyranny;
   From depths of hell your people save
   And give them vict'ry o'er the grave.
   Rejoice! Rejoice! Emmanuel
   Shall come to you, O Israel.

3. Oh, come, blest Dayspring, come and cheer
   Our spirits by your advent here;
   Disperse the gloomy clouds of night,
   And death's dark shadows put to flight.
   Rejoice! Rejoice! Emmanuel
   Shall come to you, O Israel.